MAKING SPACE CRAFT FROM JUNK

MAKING SPACE CRAFT FROM JUNK

Ready to start building some out of this world spacecraft? Let Tech-Nick, RT-1, Databot and Nano show you how.

Just copy their easy-to-follow instructions and learn all the techniques and tricks of space vehicle construction.

In this manual you'll find plenty of hints and tips to get you started. Each project can be completed from nothing more than recycled household junk, with the help of a few basic tools.

Parts In this section you will find photos of all the parts you'll need to collect, plus tips on finding alternatives to the ones shown.

Painting Learn all about adding great spray paint effects and finishing touches - plus ideas on applying the stickers found in the back of this book.

Assembly This section will show you how to construct each of the five featured spacecraft using simple step by step instructions.

Red Alert Watch out for safety alerts, especially when using sharp tools. Always ask an adult for help when advised to do so.

MAKING SPACE CRAFT FROM JUNK

CONTENTS

RT-1

With so many different plastic containers and recyclable bits and pieces around the house, it shouldn't be hard to get hold of enough parts to start building your very own spacecraft.

Ask relatives and friends to collect too. They probably use slightly different products and can be a big help when it comes to tracking down the right stuff.

THE CHOICE IS YOURS

FIND A BOX TO STORE THEM IN

Space Junk

*Never use containers that have had dangerous chemicals or medicines in them. Always ask an adult if you are not sure and remember **safety first**.*

Choosing the right glue is important. Make sure you use one that is designed for sticking plastics together. You may find that it is best to use different glues for different jobs.

It is also vital to make sure your containers are washed well in warm soapy water to remove any traces of detergent or grease. Dry them completely before attempting to build your spacecraft.

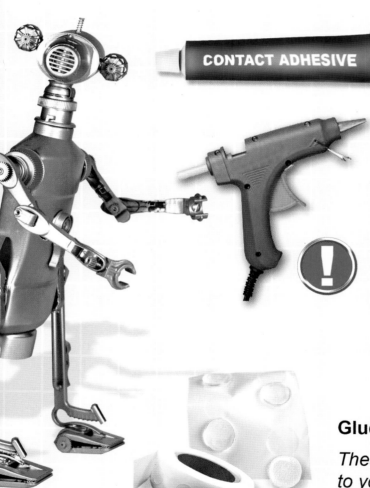

Contact Adhesive

Spread glue on both surfaces, let them dry until tacky - then press them together firmly.

Glue Gun

This device heats up the glue to make it runny. Once the glue has cooled it is very strong. Get help from an adult when using one and always wear rubber gloves to avoid getting hot glue on your hands.

Glue Spots

These are great for sticking small parts to your spacecraft. Use the permanent kind rather than removable spots.

Remove labels from containers by soaking them in water. If the glue under the label is hard to get off, use a cloth or scouring pad and cream cleaner to remove it - then rinse with clean water.

1 S-25 SHUTTLE POD

Build this nippy little Shuttle Pod using just the trigger handle of a spray bottle, two plastic clothes pegs and the caps from two water or juice bottles.

The S-25 has a crew of two and is designed for short range transportation. Powered by two Xenon drives, it manoeuvres easily and can land on rough terrain.

TOOLS

PARTS

Trigger spray bottle top with tube removed

Two clothes pegs

Two water or juice bottle caps

A junior hacksaw and glue

Don't worry if you can't find the exact same parts as the the ones shown here, our recycle droids will show you other parts that will do just as well.

1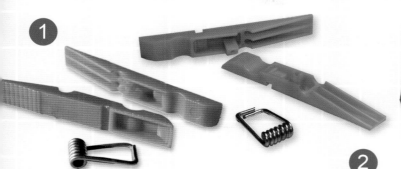

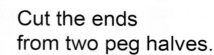

Twist apart the two pegs.

2

Cut the ends from two peg halves.

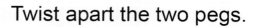

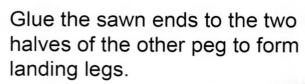

3 Glue the sawn ends to the two halves of the other peg to form landing legs.

4

Attach the legs by gluing them to the sides of the S-25 as shown.

5

TAKE YOUR TIME.
NO NEED TO FRET.
WHILE WAITING FOR
THE GLUE TO SET.

Glue on the two bottle cap engines.

Caps from marker pens make great engines.

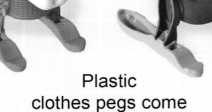

Use pen lids or rawl plugs as legs.

Plastic clothes pegs come in all sorts of varieties.

PAINT SHOP

Make sure the PVA glue is dry before spraying.

PVA Glue

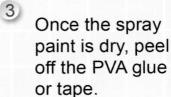

1. Mask windows of the shuttle with tape or paint over with PVA glue.

2. Hang your shuttle from a line and spray all over with paint.

3. Once the spray paint is dry, peel off the PVA glue or tape.

Spray Paint

Shake the can well and keep the spray moving - too much paint in one spot will cause messy runs.

FINISHING OFF

Use paints, tape and stickers to customise your shuttle.

Look for the sticker sheet in the back of this book.

DON'T OVERDO IT – A FEW STICKERS IN THE RIGHT PLACES WILL GIVE YOUR CRAFT AN AUTHENTIC LOOK.

When it comes to tracking down and eliminating marauding space pirates and villains, there is nothing quite like the X-90 Galaxy Defender.

Equipped with state-of-the art phaser technology it can take on all other interplanetary craft with ease.

TAKE CARE WITH SHARP TOOLS!

TOOLS

A junior hacksaw, glue and a craft knife.

PARTS

A plastic spoon

Plastic pegs

Bottle tops

A plastic bottle

Rawl plugs

Pen tops

Bendy straws

A skirt hanger

1 Glue a plastic spoon to one side of the bottle.

2 Cut the metal hook from a skirt hanger with a junior hacksaw.

3 Glue the hanger in place to form the X-90's wings.

Always cut down and away from your hands.

4 Pull two pegs apart.

5 Trim off any rough parts with a craft knife.

6 Glue the ends of one peg into the two halves of the other peg on an angle to form the X-90's legs.

7 Glue together a third leg on a shallow angle as shown with the foot facing forwards.

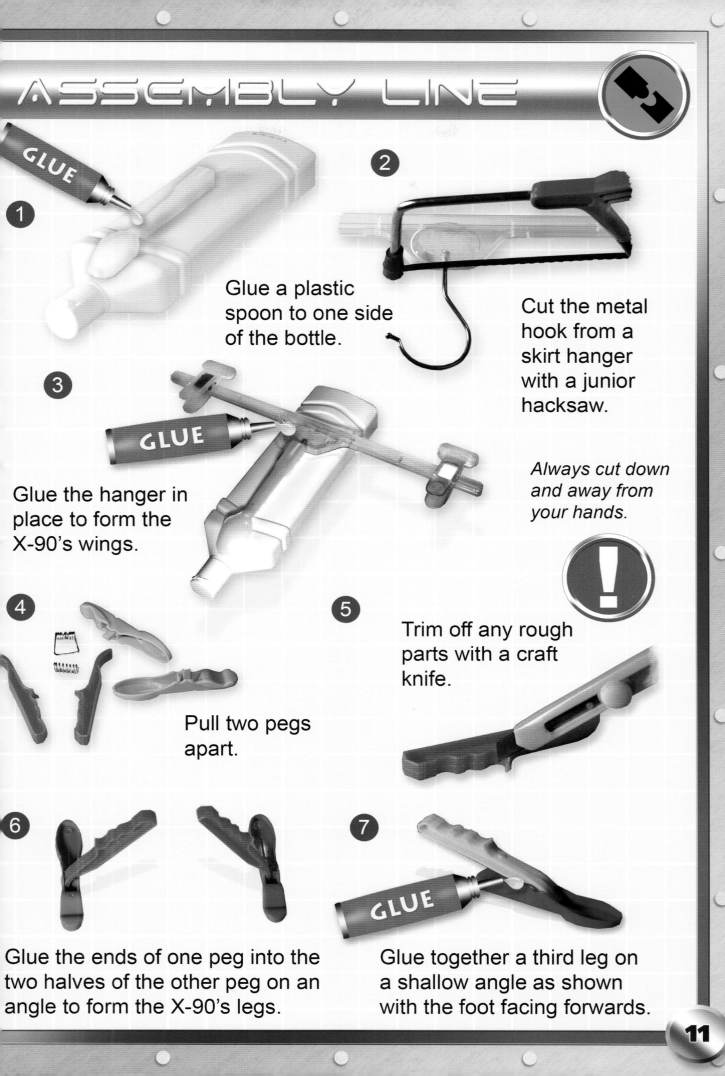

8 Glue the legs to the underside of the X-90 and wedge them in place while the glue dries.

USE PIECES OF MODELLING CLAY AS WEDGES

9 Glue the front leg in place as shown.

10 Attach two bottle top engines to the back of the X-90.

11 Glue on an assortment of pen tops and rawl plugs for weapons, engines and probes.

12 Add bendy straws for fuel pipes.

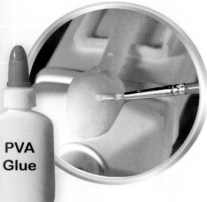

PVA
Glue

Spray
Paint

① Paint PVA glue on the window canopy and allow it to dry.

② Hang your X-90 on a line outdoors for spraying.

③ Peel off the PVA glue only when the spray paint is completely dry.

SHAKE
SHAKE
SHAKE

Spray
Paint

③ JUPITER 7

Designed for deep space exploration and long haul flights, the Jupiter 7 is a titan amongst spacecraft. It has a crew of five, four hyperon drive boosters and two ION F500 shields.

Start collecting parts and you'll be away in no time. Just three cuts with a hacksaw are all that's needed - plus a keen eye when it comes to aligning the boosters.

TOOLS

A junior hacksaw and glue.

PARTS

Four bottle tops

Four juice bottles

Three ping pong balls

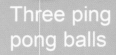

A milkshake bottle

A rawl plug, a marker top and a conical bottle top

Two coat hangers

Glue a juice bottle upside-down into the open top of the milkshake bottle.

2

Fix the other three juice bottles around the milkshake bottle making sure they are equally spaced.

tick ping
ong balls
the tops
f the three
ice bottles.

4

Glue together the conical bottle top, marker pen top and rawl plug - then fix to the top of the Jupiter 7.

Saw three ends from the plastic coathangers, making sure they are all the same size.

6 Attach the three coathanger ends to the tops of the ping pong balls and the sides of Jupiter 7 with glue.

7 Glue bottle tops to the bases of each of the main rockets.

Once the glue is perfectly strong and dry, hang up your Jupiter 7 and spray it with metallic paint. Look out for chrome effect paint which is even shinier.

DATABOT'S FACTOIDS

The Chinese were the first to build rockets over 1000 years ago. They used them in battle and gave them names like Ground Rat and Fire Dragon.

In 1903, a Russian maths teacher called Konstantin Tsiolkovsky, came up with the idea of using liquid fuel to power rockets. He dreamt of flying to the moon after reading stories by Jules Verne.

Professor Robert Hutchings Goddard launched the first liquid-fuelled rocket at Auburn in Massachusetts, USA, in 1926. It had a supersonic nozzle.

On October 3rd 1942 the German army sent up the first of its V2 rockets which could reach 128 miles above the Earth.

Sputnik I was the first man-made satellite in orbit. No bigger than a basketball, it was launched on October 4th 1957.

The first rocket to launch a person into space was the Vostok 3KA. It set off on April 12th 1961 with Yuri Gagarin aboard, who flew for 108 minutes before coming back down to Earth.

A total of 24 men flew to the moon between 1968 and 1972 aboard Saturn V rockets, each of which was over 110 metres high and weighed 3 million kilos.

Space Shuttle was a reusable spacecraft consisting of an orbiter vehicle attached to an external fuel tank and two solid rocket boosters. 135 missions were launched between 1981 and 2011.

The International Space Station is a scientific laboratory with a crew of 6 that orbits the Earth almost 16 times per day at an altitude of around 230 miles. It has had visitors from 15 different nations since 1998.

The first spacecraft to leave our solar system was Pioneer 10 which set off on March 2nd 1972, reaching speeds of 82,000 mph on its journey past the outer planets. It will arrive at the star Aldebaran 2 million years from now.

Transporting everything from fresh water to food and supplies, the Galaxy Titan can deal with an impressive payload of over sixty tons.

Cargo pods at the end of each wing can be parachuted down over drop zones where landing is hazardous.

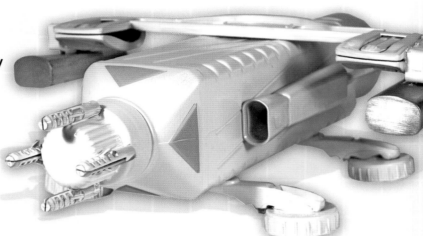

Vertical take-off is achieved using four powered landing arm that generate enough thrust to get the Galaxy Titan up to a altitude where the main rocket booster can take over.

TOOLS

A hacksaw, glue, sandpaper, wire wool, pliers and scissors.

GLUE

PARTS

Rectangular bottle

Spray can lid

Two highlighter pens

Two pegs

Four bottle tops

Two cupboard magnets

Four rawl plu

Two bendy straws

Skirt hanger

Mints

Two mi contain

Pull apart the two plastic pegs.

2

Glue each peg half to a bottle top to form legs.

3 Attach the four legs to one side of the rectangular bottle as shown.

4 Pull out the felt ink pads from the highlighter pens with pliers.

5

Cut the two bendy straws in half and discard the non-bendy ends.

6 Push a bendy straw into the top of each highlighter and glue the caps to the ends.

7 Glue the two marker pen thrusters to the sides of the Galaxy Titan.

8 Glue the spray can lid to the back of the Titan.

9 Saw the hook from the plastic skirt hanger.

10 Glue the skirt hanger to the top of the Titan about half way along the bottle.

USE PLENTY OF GLUE HERE.

20

11 Glue a cupboard magnet to the end of each wing with the magnetic end facing down.

12

Fix four rawl plugs to the nose section, making sure they are equally spaced.

I FIND MAGNETS VERY ATTRACTIVE

CARGO PODS

You can make cargo pods using small containers. Metallic mint tubs are ideal as they attach directly to the magnets on the end of the Titan's haulage arms. Plastic containers can be used if you glue on the metal plates that come with the magnets.

Use sandpaper and wire wool to remove the paint from metal containers.

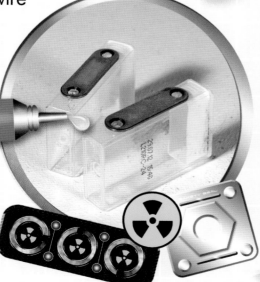

Remove labels and glue metal plates to the sides of plastic containers - then spray paint and decorate with stickers.

SPRAY BOOTH

If you are unable to hang up your spacecraft to spray it, or if the weather is bad, try making a spray booth instead.

Spray Paint

Spray Paint

ALWAYS SPRAY IN A VENTILATED WORKROOM.

Lay out newspaper and stand a large cardboard box on its side.

SUPERCRAFT

Glue can sometimes peel or become brittle in cold temperatures. If you intend to handle your spacecraft a lot, or plan on taking it to show others, it is a good idea to strengthen the joints to stop them coming apart.

PARTS & TOOLS

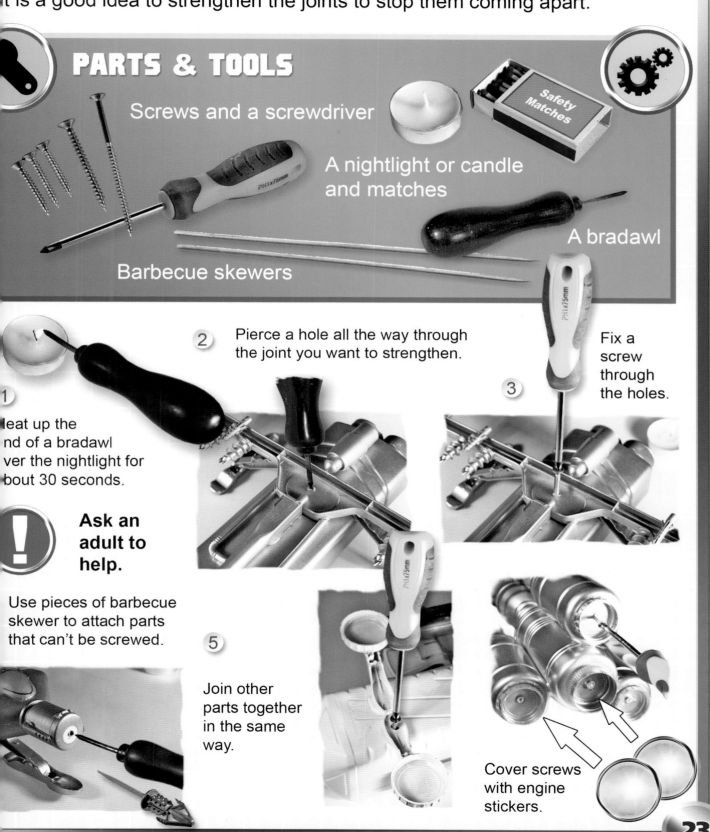

Screws and a screwdriver

A nightlight or candle and matches

A bradawl

Barbecue skewers

1
Heat up the end of a bradawl over the nightlight for about 30 seconds.

! Ask an adult to help.

Use pieces of barbecue skewer to attach parts that can't be screwed.

2 Pierce a hole all the way through the joint you want to strengthen.

3 Fix a screw through the holes.

5 Join other parts together in the same way.

Cover screws with engine stickers.

The Photon Venturer is the next generation of deep space probes, equipped with the latest technology for exploring brave new worlds.

 TOOLS

Junior hacksaw

Scissors

Bradawl

 GLUE

Glue

Nightlight

Safety Matches

Nightlight
safety matc

 **PARTS**

Two washing-up liquid bottles

Skirt hanger

3 barbecue skewer

A large
bottle top

Round
plastic
pot

Rawl plugs

Bottle caps

Ping
pong
ball

A round bottle

Cut about a third from the end of a barbecue skewer.

2

Glue two rawl plugs to the short piece of barbecue skewer as shown.

3

Glue together the round plastic tub, the top from a juice bottle, a ping pong ball and the rawl plug probe.

4

Glue the large bottle top to the cap of the round bottle.

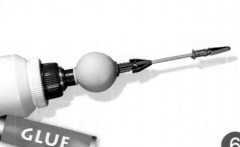

5 Now glue the nose assembly that you made at Stage 3 to the base of the bottle.

6

Cut the flip tops from the two washing up liquid bottles.

7 Heat the point of the bradawl over a nightlight flame.

8 Pierce a hole in the bottom of each washing up liquid bottle with the heated bradawl.

Get an adult to help when heating a bradawl.

9 Push a barbecue skewer all the way through each washing up liquid bottle. It may help to remove the caps to do this.

10 Glue rawl plugs to the ends of the barbecue skewers for probes.

11 Glue bottle tops to the base of eac washing up liquid bottle after mak sure that the skewers are pushed the way in.

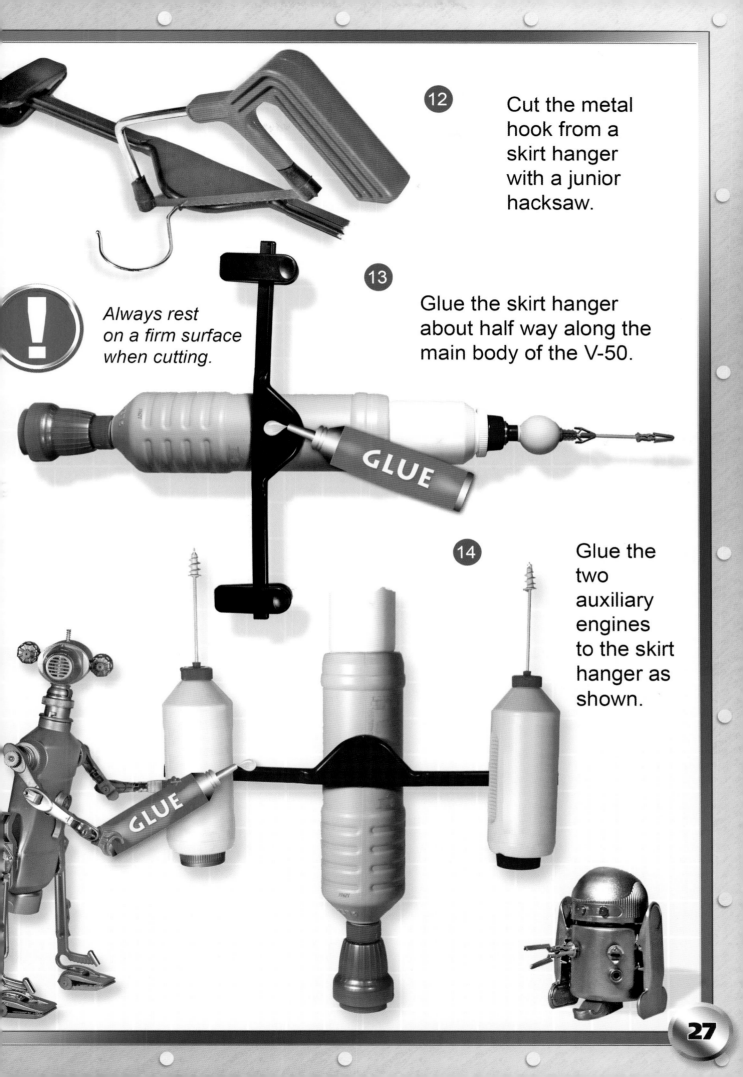

12 Cut the metal hook from a skirt hanger with a junior hacksaw.

Always rest on a firm surface when cutting.

13 Glue the skirt hanger about half way along the main body of the V-50.

GLUE

14 Glue the two auxiliary engines to the skirt hanger as shown.

GLUE

You can even make solar panels for your spacecraft using an old CD.

1. Draw a grid pattern on the shiny side of an old CD using a fine permanent marker and a ruler.

2. When the ink is dry, soak the CD in a bowl of warm water to soften the plastic.

3. Cut the CD as shown.

4. Glue a bottle top to the back for a raised mount.

Use thin nylon fishing line, or thread to hang your spacecraft from the ceiling. Polystyrene or paper mache balls, painted with acrylic paints, make great planets to hang alongside.

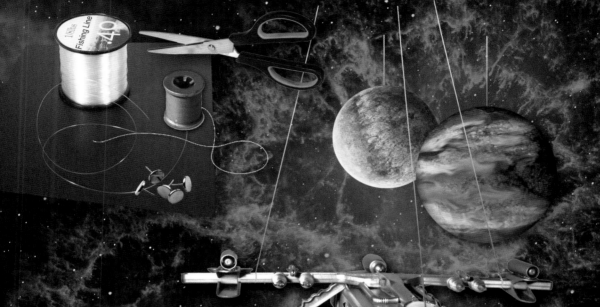

In order to keep your spacecraft balanced, tie three lines to separate parts, such as the ends of the wings and the nose section.

Glue sand and rocks to an offcut of MDF board or wood using PVA glue to create a planet surface for your spacecraft to land on.

After you have built your spacecraft, try your hand at this cool satellite dish add-on.

PARTS & TOOLS

Bendy straw

Skewer

Ping Pong Ball

GLUE

Rawl plug

Bradawl, scissors, craft knife, candle, matches and glue.

1 Cut off two pieces of skewer, each about 2cm long, and a piece of straw, about 1cm either side of the bendy section.

2 Heat a craft knife just above a candle flame - if the blade goes in the flame it will turn black and sooty.

3 Slowly and carefully slice the ping pong ball in half with the heated craft knife.

!

Ask for adult help when using a heated craft knife and bradawl.

4 Heat the tip of a bradawl just above a candle flame.

5 Pierce a hole in the centre of one half of the ping pong ball.

PIERCE A HOLE IN YOUR SPACECRAFT WHERE YOU WANT YOUR DISH TO FIT.

6 Assemble and glue the satellite dish as shown.

GLOSSARY

Acrylic paint
Fast drying paint that can be diluted in water, but is waterproof when dry.

Barbecue skewers
Long thin sticks of wood used for holding pieces of meat together while cooking.

Bradawl
A pointed tool used for making holes for screws.

Cockpit canopy
The glass window that covers the seat where a pilot sits.

Component
A part of a machine or system.

Droid
A robot in the form of a human being - short for Android.

Interplanetary
Something that goes between the planets or between planets and the sun.

Jules Verne
A French author, born in 1828, who wrote science fiction stories.

Magnesium
A strong silvery-white lightweight metal.

MDF board
Medium Density Fibreboard. A pressed board made of wood fibres, wax and resin.

Nanobot
Very tiny robots that can only be seen with a microscope.

Nightlight
A small candle in a metal holder.

PVA glue
Polyvinyl acetate. A white rubbery glue that can be mixed with water, but is waterproof when dry.

Recycle
To reuse waste materials or to change them in some way for a different purpose.

Supersonic
Faster than the speed of sound waves through air.

Xenon - *pronounced Zenon*
A colourless, odourless, heavy gas, that can be used to power spacecraft thrusters.

First published in Great Britain in 2012 by Junkcraft Books. Email info@junkcraft.com Text and Images © Junkcraft Books 2012. Stephen Munzer has asserted his rights under the Copyright, Designs and Patents Act, 1988, to be identified as the author of this work. All rights reserved. No part of this publication may be reproduced or transmitted or utilised in any form or by any means, electronic, mechanical, or otherwise, without prior permission of the publisher.

Designed and produced exclusively for Junkcraft Books.
Printed and Bound by Everbest Printing Co Ltd, China.

A CIP catalogue record for this book is available from the British Library.
ISBN 978-0-9571566-0-9

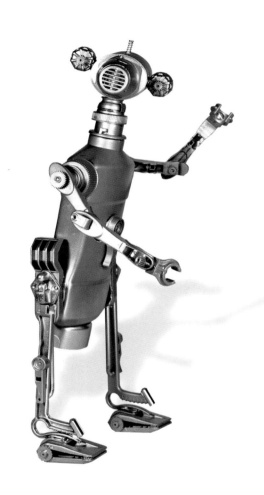

www.junkcraft.com

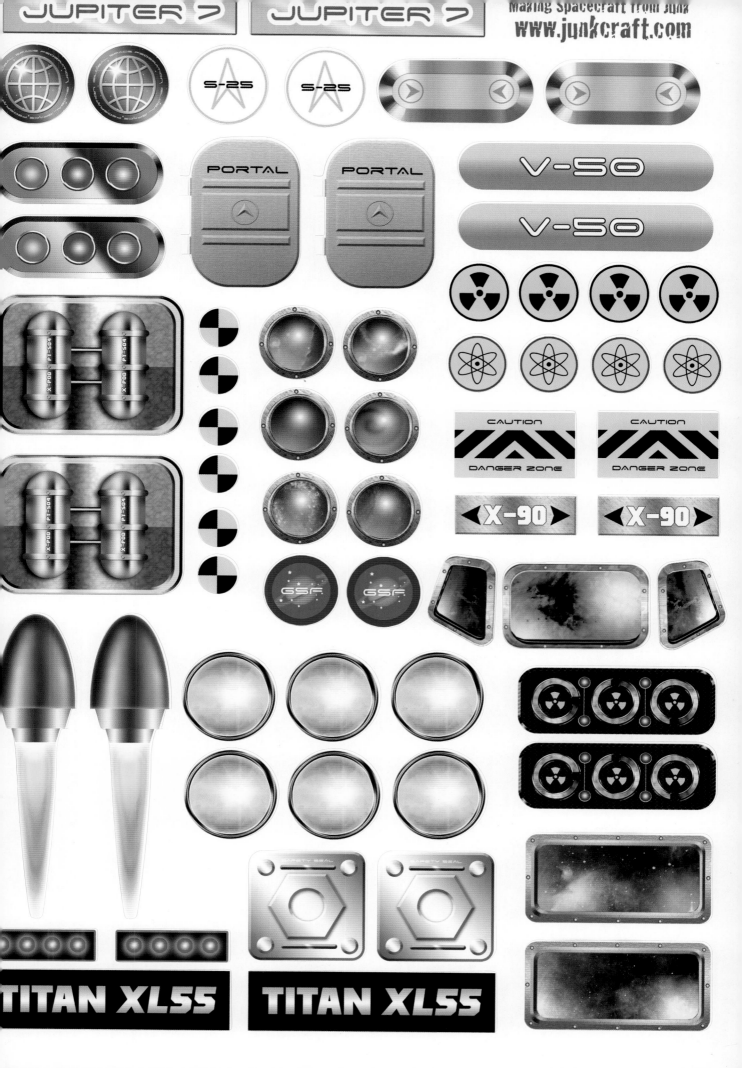